Poems of Yosemite

Here, after wandering among
these renowned mountains,
the heart grows rich with repose.

—Li Po   (AD 701–62)

ISBN: 1539724778
ISBN 13: 9781539724773
Library of Congress Control Number: 2016918212
LCCN Imprint Name: **City and State (If applicable)**

Over fifty years, I've hiked Yosemite and the High Sierra, including the six months in 1970 I spent working in the Yosemite Lodge cafeteria. My tent opened onto Tissiack (Half Dome) and most nights I would leave the tent flaps open so that I could watch the moon travel across Tissiack's face.

Yosemite is my touchstone, and when I need to reset from the pressures of life, I hike back to my youth in Yosemite's High Country.

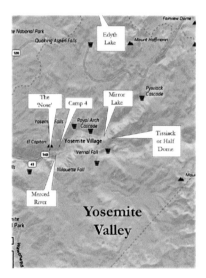

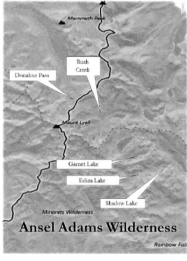

Poems

Shadow Lake

Above Shadow Lake, those twin peaks peer down as I rest;
an eerie remembrance wakes me from my weariness
as having rested on these rocks some forty years past
and having captured that then moment in memory.

A mnemograph of lake, trail, sky; of hopes, fears, self.
Twin selves reflected in apposition:
What distance between same place?
What sameness with distant self?

A faded image etched in now silvered neurons
retouched by these Sierran hues. My older palate
savors the bittersweet of the distance traveled.
A world before self, now a self before world.

I continue to the lake and touch my lips to its surface to sip.
Before, I opened my eyes and saw but myself reflected;
now I am shadowed as one with the mountains above.

Tissiack's Tears

[F]or I was absorbed in the great Tissiack [Half Dome]—I have
gazed on Tissiack a thousand times—in days of solemn storms,
and when her form shone divine with the jewelry of winter, or
was veiled in living clouds; and I have heard her voice of winds,
and snowy, tuneful waters when floods were falling; yet never did
her soul reveal itself more impressively than now.
                                                        —John Muir

Tissiack's tears fall from her rain-stained face,
her profile one with the lichened rock.
She, the spirit of the Ahwahneechees,
speaks silently with the voice of winds
and whispered waters from her cleft crown.

My tent at the Lodge opened to her,
and for six months I gazed upon her face –
divine dawns, evening clouds and moon-full nights –
but I was youth and distracted
and unaware as to that unrevealed.

Forty years later, I return to her
and sit in the moonlight at Mirror Lake.
As my eyes tire and become unfocused,
I see her missing half in the water—
her half that isn't, her mystic moiety.

She then whispers of unhalves, and in the
rippled, reflective waters appears
my unhalf—those thoughts, unthought and
that life, unlived. I too shed tears
and share her now revealed soul.

Tissiack's Tears by Alden Trevor McWilliams.
(www.aldentmcwilliams.com.)

The 'Nose' is the part of El Capitan that projects into Yosemite Valley.

Camp 4

'If I die, I die.'
The realness of those words
sent a shiver down my spine
as I listened to the climbers.
It was late autumn, 1969.
There was a pause after his words
and each face made the slightest nod
peering deeply into the flames;
Tom Bauman had just soloed the Nose.

Slowly, I began to put pitons into
the face of life, jammed my fist
into fissures, and ascended slowly.
I delighted when my blood dripped
onto the dark diorite veins in the granite.
For this is life and I believe
in the challenge of the ascent and
the use of a life to outlive it.

It is now the winter of 2014, and
I wander through Camp 4.
I look at the young, intense faces
as they to peer into the flames.
I would share with them what
has been my own first ascent,
but Tom lives on, so I scream
to a startled camp my tribute to life:
         'If I die, I die.'

Merced River, 1992

As we canoe the bend,
the aeried osprey
takes one downbeat
and soars 'cross river.

The moment transcends,
and we extract
an etched memory
of a river'd still life.

Time and river
flow in continua,
yet only from moments
do memories build.

And by and from these,
do we conjoin
ourselves
to remembered past.

Find the Wild

Where to go to wrest life's conflicts,
that somewhere, someplace to recuse?
When one feels that within's without
and ere conclusion, now confused.

My parents taught me, "Find the Wild,"
and use it as mine own compass.
Oft I've journeyed back within
and found a troubl'd soul's solace.

But for our own we've not bequeathed
a comparable cultural meme.
Where shall our kids find themselves?
Where shall they go to self-redeem?

For our largess is numbing tech,
mere distractions of compute.
Will our children find the switch
to effect their own soul's reboot?

Edyth Lake

Of time — it ceased its frenzied headlong rush
as Edyth Lake was then as ever been,
too far away from trail to bring the now
a perfect place to travel deep within.
Cross-country'd hack through manzanita bush
to mountain tarn of no especial fame
except it offered undisturbed place
for me to meditate and self reclaim.
I set up camp in Edyth's only copse
beshadowed by the reach of Nance's Peak
no sign of fire nor ever man's imprint
and no encumbrance to distract the week.

A fishing rod but little else I brought
for summer's trout and berries should sustain
allowing mind to unencumbered search
as far within as ere it may attain.
Released to reach without a bounded leash;
too seldom does the mind unfettered go—
a puppy, cautious sniffed and stepped from cage
does grow emboldened to explore and know.
After several days my thoughts flowed into
a deep recess amid the granite scree
a peacefulness reflecting light and peak—
a lake I found that still engenders me.

About Someday

I will be here someday,
    when we will share thoughts;
I will be there someday,
    where time meets mountains.
But I'll be here before,
    writing about someday.

Fishing

Some live for the dry fly,
dancing where riffle meets eddy
and that visceral anticipation
as to what lies below.

But for me: paper—clear and flat
as a lake—awaiting a subconscious
thought to rise from the depths, to strike
and enable these lines.

If There's Not

If there's not,
        there should be;
No worries;
        we'll invent
Whatever it is
        we don't need.

Cosmic Hiss

From the beginning,
from the Big Bang,
comes the hiss.

Its soft sound surrounds,
whispering with
sibilance:

"This Earth—Our Eden;
don't blow it."

Across Garnet Lake

The sun renews, and the view
across Garnet Lake looks
like a coffee-table book.

Though this is quite real—less I feel
than with such book on couch
and winter's winds without.

Darkness Deems

Silence succumbs us to see;
with listening, what Is appears;
the darkness deems that we hear
with closed eyes, the harmonies.

Selectionist Proclaim

Darwinist:	"I exist because God selects."
Creationist:	"I exist because God chooses."
Existentialist:	"I exist because I choose."
Selectionist:	"I exist because I select."

My head spins in the muddle
of a Devonian muddy puddle,
where ancestors wiggled and writhed,
thence to land and hence reside.

But the list above makes one wonder
as brain and heart rend asunder
for a meaning upon which to stand,
wobbling, as if fin'd on land.

My aim: Selectionist proclaim,
now sits atop the idea food chain.
For only by our own selection
do we discover our own election.

Is Nothing

Birth – Something from nothing.
Death – Something to nothing.

Does the coroner ever say,
"Someone died of nothing."?
Still I fear,
Nothing will kill Me.

So I search for something
Yet uncomprehending that –
Something is Nothing,
Is Everything.

Darwin and Dasein

From which perspective, human action originates.
—Heidegger

Quite the same, really—
aspects of one
as energy and matter
or space and time.

Expression from substrate,
effusion from source—
so much energy comes
of matter's conversion.

We become by Darwin
but Be by Dasein—
that single syncretism,
of our Design.

Garnet Lake

I pause to listen to the silence –
I am one with the million befores
and the afters and at great peace
amid the soundless, immense harmonies.

I become the rhythm of the spheres
and part of that oneness orchestration,
both absorbed and apart in a light,
too orderly to be but blind chance.

There must be purpose to the whole
that transcends reason and goes beyond
the despair of nothing. I become the Cosmos
not the chaos and within I am part.

There is a miracle to existence
and its exquisite, ephemeral beauty.
To hike to Garnet Lake is to be without,
wherein, without, I find my within.

Morning Moon

The morning moon reflexes
east, surrounded in pink
and luminescent dawn,
and rests upon the peaks.

I could look toward sunrise
with its bright,
gleaming source for the
iridescence in the west.

But I don't—
for the moon
reflexes me
in vision'd reverie:

Light and beauty
attenuating to
vague forms and fading
across time and distance.

Sierran Stream

There was nothing better
than coming upon a Sierran stream,
soaked in sweat and throat parched.
Lying flat, I kissed a small pool
to imbibe its divine nectar.

   That was in my teens.

Now I take out my water filter
and plunge one end into the water,
the other into my plastic bottle.
I pump and then drink—the water
has a slight propylene taste.

Yosemite Valley

The Valley is,
      because it isn't;
El Capitan is,
      because it is –
But my Miwok basket is,
      because it's both.

Tribute to Honnold

Right foot into this little dimple that you can toe in on
aggressively so it's opposing the left hand, then you can,
like, zag over across to this flat, down-pulling crimp that's
small but you can bite it.
　　　　[From Honnold's climbing notebook.]

　　　For me, the most transcendental feat –
　　　Your smeared soles at Freeblast Slabs,
　　　your shoulder jammed into Offwidth
　　　and cardiac-kick at the Boulder were:
　　　　　　Inspirational; unimaginable.

　　　We sit in theatre chairs white-gripping
　　　our armrests and, too often, eyes closed.
　　　Up on El Cap as much as we'll e'er be,
　　　We twist our bodies in synchrony.
　　　We've seen how immeasurable
　　　the possible; the achievable
　　　of the inconceivable. At last,
　　　an image beyond the past; a hero
　　　of no vanquished enemy,
　　　brawling limitless potentiality.
　　　Following your lead, we reimagine
　　　how we might ascend our valley'd lives.

I am Rush Creek

The river flows with its own will, but the flood is bound by the banks.
 If it were not thus bound, its freedom would be wasted.
                    —Vinoba Bhave

I am Rush Creek. I conjoin two forks:
one drains Marie Lakes below Mount Lyell,
the other, melted snows from Donahue Peak.

I sault into Waugh Lake; spillover
into a chain of lush, grassy meadows;
and saunter into Gem Lake where I rest.

From here I flow in channels and tunnels
and dolefully disembogue into Mono Lake,
a terminal lake with no exit.

I do not rue this, my prescribed course,
and though I am Rush Creek, I am not,
for I am its waters.

Ever renewed—the waters become me and I them
as chortling cascades, reflective eddies, and trout
sparkling in luminous pools.

And because I am bounded, I can be what I am—
Rush Creek. I am perpetual, and time
flows through me as water.

Nisenan youth made a spiritual journey into the High Sierra mountains where they would camp alongside a river or waterfall until they heard in their dreams their "river's song." Returning to the village, each youth then sang his song which determined the role he would play in the tribe.

The poem is meant to be chanted to the first ninety-eight measures of the Second Movement of Beethoven's Seventh Symphony. The starting measure number is indicated in parenthesis above each stanza.

The River's Voice

Hard day of hiking,
camp by the river,
roll out my sleeping bag,
lay down to rest.
Sleep won't release me,
drawn into the singing stream,
softly so faintly
I hear the river's voice.
(19)
Sounds of the spirits,
riffles from the river,
heard by the Nisenans
aeons ago.
Braves on their journey
stayed the night where I now lay,
listened for their river words
became whom the voices say.
(35)

Sounds presemantic,
heart hears and understands,
words that are not words
thoughts that can't be thought.
Words displace twilight,
the senses enlighten me,
mountains echo melodies
spirits fill the night.
(51)
Hear not with my ears,
listen only with my mind,
no, not with the mind
only hear with my heart—
ears may only hear the words,
mind may only think its thoughts,
spirit of the river's words
embrace me with sound.
(67)
Listen as a mountain cirque
echo within my emptiness,
imagining a Nisenan youth
becoming whom I hear.
Fill in my hollowness
with the tune the river plays,
dancing to harmonies
showing me the way.
(83)
Enspelled by the river's song,
hours eddy in the flow,
confused if I am still awake
or voice is in my dreams.
At dawn, I put on my pack,
hike back to the John Muir trail—
I have become my path
the river's voice prevails.

Wise Man

Wise Man, which, in a life well spent
are your moments of repent?
Nay, rather, which do you recall
as the memories above them all?

For I stand in my own conceive
and into future wrest perceive;
now is the time for me to try
to learn from those who have lived wise.

Should I live without construct
and treat my time as usufruct?
Or design ever with purpos'd plan,
what makes in end the better man?

"Both and not be my answer
embrace each as would a dancer;
be thoughts simple and reflective of
the blessing to have live life's loves."

Lodgepole Pine

Torque yourself to the earth;
feel your threads grab the soil;
then bury deeper as
each tightening gyre takes hold.
Be like the lodgepole pine,
with striated sinews
that withstand winter's winds.
Those who grow straight and tall
do fall too easily.
In the end, your bleached ribs
should lie twisted, gnarled
as the lodgepole pine.

Earth Shadows

We are Earth shadows,
evolved from the umbra
into the penumbra,
supposing sunlight.

We are our terrible twos,
as independence indicts,
and we shout and pout
to no purpose.

For we are still of Earth,
and our whines annoy
our parent who now
scarcely tolerates.

We are Earth's shadows
and must hope she
is more loving of us
than we of her.

In 1970, my job at Curry Co., Yosemite Lodge was Cold Supply. I arrived each morning at 5:00 a.m. to pack the ice in the cafeteria displays, prepare the juice and fruit and make the coffee. The best part about Cold Supply is that I finished work after lunch service and would hike most afternoons.

Mountain Dew - 1970

From the car, they tossed the can
an empty can of Mountain Dew;
it nearly hit me as I walked,
to my job as kitchen crew.

Stunned, I shouted words of scorn
to which their laughs were my reply.
They sped away in trail of smoke,
dismissive of my concerned cry.

I asked as I retrieved the can,
should I not admonish act?
Should we not take every step
To counteract man's impact?

And as I prepped the breakfast fare
I asked the grapefruit if they knew,
'how provisional our presence here
and tenuous man's purview?'

'Unless thence to change your ways,
You'll waste until you're through—
for Nature always has her day,
that's what the mountains do?'

Fust

Who is it who fusts within?
Who raised hand as child but never chosen,
so simpers in the silent, sleepless hours.
Who, if sought, hides as fetal'd child
under the covers of consciousness.

Who, in lieu, grows in this fallowed plot?
And appears as apparition when asked:
"Who are you?" More, what shall we do
with the empty womb within all
that cries out for conception?

There Comes a Moment

There comes a moment in the fall
when life turns cold,
and leaves lie frosted
a hoary'd silver,
and trees reach upwards
arthritic fingers
as summer's hopes
have since dehisced.

The moment chills
through to marrow,
and its realization
completes remorse.
For hereon, winter drifts
past solstice, beyond solace,
leaving all
in shivering solitude.

Within Stone

I can't write what can't be written,
but I can write what it is not—
a sculpture within stone.

It is not that which is sensed
nor those thoughts that can be thought—
the enigma of a koan.

The following was written for a friend upon being told that his cancer had metastasized throughout his body.

Beyond Hope

Beyond hope is not nothing—

The twin stars of existence
    collapse into each other
        creating that black hole
            which is less than nothing.

All light sucked within
    but light is energy
        which by being absorbed
            sustains the something.

Do, friend, for by so doing
    defies your fugacious fate
        which is not nothing
            but everything.

Donahue Pass

I broke camp well before the morning sun
reached Donahue Peak
and hiked up Rush Creek toward the pass.

The sky was still a deep turquoise
with only a vapor trail marking the otherwise
perfect blue.

I compared this transverse on foot
with my many vapored crossings—
and how different.

As passenger, my crossed legs
cramp during hours of
flight inactivity.

Today, they as well cramp
but from mere miles
of overexertion.

How else can I compare passenger to hiker?
As passenger, my goal is to arrive;
this week, I search just for where I've been.

I break out above the tree line, and
the strength of the Sierran sun
glares off the exfoliating granite.

This midlife expedition is
a chance to reflect—
a solitary soliloquy.

The trail steepens, and the heaviness of the pack
tires me quickly. I stop and look back
into the Ansel Adams Wilderness.

My thoughts have randomly traveled
this week through time as a search
through a disordered drawer of photographs.

And despite my many maps,
I have not yet found the trail that leads
from one picture to another.

How shall I link these life images?
Am I the same in each
or, in each, the difference?

Is each a reflection from within?
Or from without?
Has perspective created the persona?

I reach ten thousand feet and
labor for breath from
the thinness of air.

I am burdened by the injunction:
To know thyself,
and in this, I stumble.

At my age, shouldn't I know
whether I am
the hiker or passenger?

Am I one and not the other,
or am I both, still unreconciled?
A kaleidoscope turned by time.

Perhaps not one nor both
but neither—
a chameleon to and of circumstance.

Upon a shoulder ridge,
I lean my pack upon scattered scree.
A short but steep distance remains.

Is my pursuit a Euro-ruse?
Have I been duped again into banging rocks
and crying out for snipe of self?

A vast cultural conspiracy perpetuating
philosophical fraud? More,
have all such expeditions been misbegotten?

My breath is now tortured,
and my legs spasm under pack as
I agonize the last switchbacks.

I start to realize I'm as metamorphic
as these granite slabs that simply reflect
the changing light of the Sierran sky.

I am, after all my travels,
not the subject but the object
in my life's sentence.

And from this anaerobic epiphany
comes a surge of lightness
and buoyancy from burden shed.

I rest several minutes at the crest,
separating these watersheds. Hereon,
my thoughts flow in the direction traveled.

I have crossed Donahue Pass
and no longer labor up its perpetual incline –
I exult in the ease of my descent.

When You Camp

When you camp upon a granite slab
the night is long and soreful;
besides listening for the bears,
one finds mindgames to exploreful:
Some things defined by what they are
and some by what they're not;
moreover, some are because they're not,
yet others not because they are.
There I am that by what I am
and here by what I'm not;
for what I'm not is because I am;
at last dawn has reached the peaks.

Why, If Not?

"Why, if not?" I presume to ask
to no one but a Jeffrey Pine
who haply heard my quiet query
there by stream, where rest reclined.

The Pine responded with a sigh
that wafted as words of wind:
Nature doesn't choose to answer,
adjures instead to find within.

Terms

As I watch the gibbous moon
luminesce
        off glacier'd granite,
I look into her eyes
        and tell God,
that I accept her terms
        with grace.

There Is no We

There is no We,
just us.

Us,
in our Marmot sleeping bags,
watching and shivering
as the Sierran storm
tears trees in half.

Where is the We
in this wrath?

But even, whither the I?
Wishing, only,
amid the fury,
there is a me.

To my mother, Zippy, for reading Seuss, Lear, Milne, Carroll and so many others to me as a child. Robert Frost understood that, 'the intonation of the speaking voice carries more meaning than particular words.' Perhaps, still, in this culture of noise, reading out loud will instill in our kids a love for the musicality of the English language.

The Hunting of the Not

—In two Fits—

Fit the First

I hear a rumor of a rare Not sighting
near Ediza lake,
so I gather my boots, a pack, a jar,
and a frosted coconut cake.

For Nots are elusive and hide anywhere,
but of coconut, they're particularly fond.
Perchance by putting the cake in my jar,
I can entice the Not to respond.

As I stand at the trailhead holding my cake,
who but a baker hikes by;
"What was I planning to do with my cake?"
He asks without meaning to pry.

"I'm off to Ediza to capture a Not,"
an interest he seems not to share.
"Do you mind if I join you? I'm heading up there
'cause I need the high-mountain air."

"You see," he continues, "I'm a baker by trade,
but my pancakes have never had fluff,
so I've brought my sourdough starter and flour
and the rest of my bakery stuff."

"If I can come," he offers, "I'll treat you to pancakes,
which you'll find are remarkably rare;
at ten thousand feet, batter bubbles better,
making pancakes lighter than air."

We agree and together commence up the trail
though we both look quite out of place—
I balance in hand my coconut cake,
while a grill does our baker embrace.

We hike several miles, then sit to rest
when on the trail a ranger appears.
He looks at us both, then the cake and the grill,
and decides that something is weird.

"Why are you carrying these things that you have?"
He asks, so we had to explain.
"Pancakes! Nots! These are my passions!"
His eagerness could not be contained.

"Join us," I offer, for we'll find him quite helpful
as I had not, a Not-hunting license;
plus, the lake is hidden, away from the trail,
so can use his backcountry guidance.

"Nots are tricky," he says, as we continue to climb,
"for they are not where you think they should be,
but I've never tried frosted coconut cake,
this is something I just have to see."

"Nots," he proceeds, "are certainly quite rare
and sit atop our endangered list.
Remarkable, as the fact of it all,
we're not sure if they even exist."

We huff up hundreds of dry, dusty switchbacks
and arrive with the setting of sun.
"The air is perfect," the baker proclaims
and soon his setup is done.

The ranger and I hike over a ridge
where he raises his binoculars.
He searches for something not resembling a Not
as I cram coconut cake in my jar.

For a Not is not, whatever you think,
nor seen if you're looking for Nots,
so we search for a place to locate our jar,
and find what is not a Not spot.

We return to camp to find that our baker
has finished prepping his dough.
In the high air, it does bubble better
and froths as if ready to blow.

We crawl in our tents and listen to silence
that may have been Nots in the night;
we awake as the crags of Ritter and Banner
inflame with the first rays of light.

The baker pours grease upon his large grill
and lights a great fire below;
he splashes on water and when the drops dance,
ladles batter as is so apropos.

The batter sizzles forming big bubbles,
with holes the size of Swiss cheese,
but what happens next, makes us all gasp—
for the pancakes float away on a breeze.

Yes, the pancakes while cooking upon the hot grill
became so light from the air and the heat,
they float away like helium balloons
seconds before they are ready to eat.

Each batch flies off like a flock of Pine Warblers
circling o'er our heads as we stare,
then around the lake, carrying the crags
and off to somewhere out there.

After all of our pancakes have thus flown away,
the baker is delighted to say:
"At least they are fluffy; no doubt about that"
and declares it a wonderful day.

But we are still hungry and pour syrup upon
what remains of our Not coconut cake;
we traipse then over to our special Not spot
alongside the shore of the lake.

We discover the clump of cake is all gone
so I screw the lid on quite tight.
The ranger and I looked in at our Not.
"It is beautiful," we cry with delight.

Nothing forms friends as well as a quest,
and we laugh all the way back to our cars.
Now, thereupon my living room mantle
stands my rare Not-specimen jar.

Fit the Second

I settle down with wine and a book
to enjoy a midwinter's eve,
when I glance from my reading to look at my Not,
"Oh no," for then I perceive:

The Not's jar lid is slightly ajar
which I refix and lift to the light;
I turn it sideways, then upside down,
but, no doubt: My Not's taken flight.

I quickly dial an emergency number,
to alert the authorities;
it is one thing for Nots to roam near Ediza
but of concern in a major city.

A sergeant answers with Gallic gruffness,
"Monsieur, what, again is amiss?"
His pen poses over a long-duplexed list
with an attitude of pure parti pris.

"A Not," he exclaims, "*très sérieux*,
I must alert *mes* superiors!"
He puts down the phone and hurries away;
a commotion was then overheard.

"We have to issue an APB
to all police, fire and vice;
what unique feature should we describe?"
"Can't be seen." There, said it thrice.

Mere minutes later a police car drives up,
without lights nor even a sound;
the inspector takes pictures of the jar on the mantle
for clues that may possibly be found.

He scans for footprints left in the dust,
then goes for a roll of crime tape.
He makes a squiggly outline in yellow,
asking, "Is this the Not's actual shape?"

"Yes," I answer, "though it's only a guess,
as Nots have never been seen."
"I see," he mutters writing some notes,
then summons his forensics team.

There are always reporters monitoring crime
who now gather outside my front door;
their microphones on and cameras primed,
"An interview, please!" they implore.

"Where did I find my now famous Not?
And did I have a license to keep?
Am I aware how dangerous it is
for a Not to be roaming our streets?"

"Save our children!" a young mother cries,
"and what to do if attacked?"
"Bathe your kids," I say in reply,
"in a tub of vanilla extract."

There was lots of Not news and, to add color,
Not experts were all interviewed;
videos were needed of the famous Not spot,
so to Ediza hiked television crews.

Still everyone worries, wonders, waits,
and watches where a Not wouldn't hide;
we even try frosted coconut cake
but nothing, though we look far and wide.

While everyone searches at everywhere not,
they discover the world of nonthings—
the interstices and the spaces between—
much amazed by the things never seen.

A wondrous world opens for them—
of the myriad of things not there;
"I had no idea that all of this wasn't,"
posed a lawyer pointing up in the air.

The mayor, because of the Not,
places his possessions out onto the curb.
"I felt claustrophobic," he then tells the press,
"with nothing, I'm quite undisturbed."

One evening I return after searching all day
and notice the lid was askew;
my Not has returned to go back to Ediza,
after converting the town to her view.

I ask my good friends if they'll join me again,
and with relish they quickly agree;
the baker then offers, "I've a surprise for you both,
for I've concocted a new recipe."

We hug at the trailhead, then head up the trail,
in my hands is my special Not jar;
the baker carries a convection oven
and the ranger, his binoculars.

Halfway, while resting, I query the baker,
"How shall you keep your pancakes secure,
so as to not fly off again like Pine Warblers?"
"Unleavened batter," our baker assures.

At the not Not spot, we open the top,
and a light breeze whistles by me;
we bless the time we had with our Not,
for she *wasn't* a Boojum, you see.

Dining in front of the convection oven,
we eat pancakes far harder than bark
but agree our adventure was far better fun
than if we were hunting a Snark.

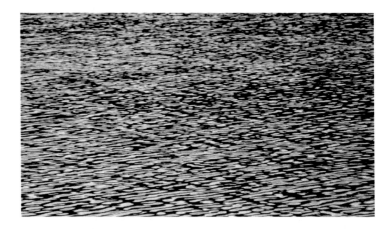

Sequoia

Ineffable –
Still I write these lines
                trite.

A scaffold of words
which whence removed
casts only a silence
of long shadows.
To you, the paradigm
of living time,
I write ephemeral
                wordless words.

You say nothing
though the wind wafts
words which speak
beyond words to each.
The sound of wind
continues in the stillness
and reaches into
the logos which
spells the visitors
                deeper than these.

You speak centuries –
the entire time
of our adolescence –
when you've watched
as we wrestle with
the worst of nature.
You were made for fire
and your cambium grows
thick bark and fibers
                over the scars.

Does too our tissue
grow over scars?
Wars, devastations?
Will these as well clear
the understory?
But you don't create fire
you endure it.
Is that the difference?
This is your nature,
                    share and compare us ours.

We see your exposed rings
and the markers
telling us which ring
belongs to Christ
and the Inquisition.
I see my ring
but not the current
as only the living
scribe those rings
                    and they are being written.

Poetry overcomes time
and endows the ephemeral
with permanence.
Your permanence
is presence and in
this silence of time
the visitors sense
then understand –
they've come not to see you
                    but themselves.

Below Cathedral Peak

Alone, I camp below Cathedral Peak –
God, I know you're not whom we say you are
and you should have a good case for slander.
What fantastical tales we tell of you –
and the more nonsensical, I wonder,
absurdly, makes you more believable.
As the night sky ascends from below
until only the mountain's white peak glows,
I perpend how you are our double-bind –
Antithetical, yet inevitable;
omnipotent, yet shirking the onus
of sin, disease and immorality.

I have back-tracked my last fifty years
from the convenience of nihilism
and of nullity which once embraced me;
I loved that luxury of arrogance
and conceit to everywhere forswear faith.
Over years, I've shed those simple vestments
to now plea the argument's opposite –
But not Faith. What emerged is a mountain
from igneous intrusion and ascend'd
within until it now glows as beacon.

I, a conjoined blind man with elephant
unable to wrest the entirety,
but these mere three aspects of your being:
I do know of your love; your love of beauty
and your love of life. These would and could not
Not otherwise emerge from the darkness
and the absolute void of space.
Nullity is too facile and stays so
unless there's more – More, for black begets black
and cannot create something from nothing.

And one should grow old without seeing
that there is something; that an is, Is;
a wisdom and grace that originates.
It is hard to deny both denial
and a god who cares for prayer, penitence
and sacrifice. Here, below Cathedral Peak,
an epiphanic edifice, I see
a parent god who prods and acclaims her
progeny's progress and accomplishments.
It is enough for us to inhale the
thin air of her love transcribed and written
into a new and blessed scripture
for both child and parent to embrace

Made in the USA
Coppell, TX
07 September 2020